DANCING SOBER

Memoirs & Poems

by

Maria Boldreghini

ISBN 978-0-6151-7937-7

For John

My dance in life continues to blossom from your love and encouragement.

Dedicated to:

My parents, Charles & Catherine Boldreghini

Without these two loving people in my life, life's lessons of faith, laughter, adversity, giving, and accepting, would have been lost in the mire.

and

Two beloved family members, Russell Hilt and Jimmie Joe Ward

Whose lost lives remain dear to my heart, whose humor I remember and smile, whose life stories and spirits help me remain sober.

Not lonely, but alone is
My life –
My own predestined complacency,
Self-understood

When I was young
So very young
A bird sang sweet
Melodies all day
The sun warmed my
Senses and thoughts

Thoughts were endless
Of love and goodness
Fear not a part of my being
So far away was my
Future of despair and confusion
A mind immune to such
Heartache, void of loss

Now a constant battle for
Me and the other
Between me and all others
For is it the promised land or
The land without promise that
I yearn for to save
My heart and soul

My Story

I am an alcoholic. Plain and simple, I loved the drink. I still do, but I haven't had a drink in many years. When I quit drinking, I thought I would never *dance* again. I was wrong. Drinking to me was just a part of my life. No, it was my life. My first memories of drinking were having a few drinks around the age of 10 with a girlfriend. We'd sneak beers from her parent's fridge and mix it with orange juice after everyone else was asleep. The cheap version of a mimosa I suppose. I didn't really like the taste of it, but it was something we weren't supposed to do so that made it attractive. What I didn't realize at that young age was those early drinks had awoken a sleeping alcoholic monster with an insatiable appetite for personal and spiritual destruction. Years later, my dance with that monster began.

Drinking for me was escaping reality. I abused alcohol because on a conscious level, the "high" was a release, a release of feelings, a release of responsibilities, a release into my own private, safe, intoxicated world. This was the only world I wanted to know. The only world I felt comfortable in. I simply fell in love with drinking, and it was not until I became sober that I realized what I loved most was actually the escapism involved in drinking. Getting high on alcohol took me to places where I had never been before. Places where I felt safe and secure, alive and loved. And the friends! My, how easy it was to make friends. And the only requirement to be my friend was to be able to share a barstool with me and engage in some deep, philosophical, going nowhere conversation colored with humor. Drinking became my vehicle that drove me wild.

I had heard once that in trying to determine if you might be an alcoholic you should consider not so much what you drink or how often you drink, but *why* you drink. I drank to get drunk. I got drunk to escape life as it was. And it wasn't that my life was that awful, it was just life-less. For as long as I can remember, I could always feel a pain inside. Where this pain or sadness came from, I never knew and I never really gave it much thought, I just felt it. They say misery loves company and thru alcohol, my pain found a companion. So I drank to get drunk so I could get to that point where there was only me and my pain. No one else could enter this world, no one else was allowed to sense my pain. For then, I would have to explain it and by explaining it, would have to own it and do something about it.

Non-alcoholics drink to get drunk at times too but they are not looking to escape something, but to just "blow it out" and have a good time. *Normal* drinkers go to a party and want to drink to catch that buzz to really relax and let go. I could be totally wrong about that because I was never a normal drinker. It's just a hunch. This alcoholic would go to a party and already be buzzed by the time I got there. I remember drinking entire bottles of wine or at least 3-4 hefty gin & tonics just while I was getting ready to go out. My *why* for drinking was totally different and totally personal. It was definitely *not* a social thing. It was a very private affair with the bottle. As with most love affairs, the feeling of wanting to be with it, thinking about it all day when away from it, and rushing into its arms once home, my affair was no different. And years later, the growing guilt I felt about it was no different either. Sobriety brings with it such clarity of hindsight.

The first year of my recovery from alcoholism was extremely painful, physically and emotionally. I hated anyone who could drink. I was angry, irritable and frustrated almost daily. I had dreams of drinking. I think the worst feeling of withdrawal was when I wanted to drink so badly, my "skin would crawl." I never really understood this phrase before I quit drinking. You just feel like you are literally about to jump out of your skin. And when I would share this in an Alcoholics Anonymous (AA) meeting, I would see so many heads just nodding. I could sulk, cry, act like a baby in those meetings because my alcoholic pacifier had been taken away and no one thought of me as weak or crazy. Everyone understood. It was truly the only place during that first year where I felt *normal*. Those were the only people who truly understood what I was going through. So I hung around in those meetings for quite some time.

I wanted sobriety so badly that I told myself to just do whatever it took. As much as my close friends and family supported me during this time, I couldn't turn to them for help. If I shared with a non-alcoholic about my skin crawling, I wouldn't get that comforting nod of understanding. Instead, I would see this quizzical look on the other person's face, and I imagined that person thinking, "Man, I'm glad I'm not an alcoholic, what the hell is she talking about?" Not to say that's what they *were* thinking, but that's just what I thought in my confused state of sobriety. So I only trusted the opinion of other recovering alcoholics and began to trust in my God again to give me the strength to battle this life altering event I hadn't marked on my calendar.

That's a big part of how I got sober, AA meetings and God. What brought me to the point of wanting sobriety is a little more difficult to explain. Once my dependency took over, each year the *symptoms* of my drinking became progressively worse. The hangovers were more and more intense, no matter what I had drunk the night before or how much. That alcoholic, pontificating monster inside me became so scary that even I was afraid to confront it. The blackouts were more often and intense. Blackouts are extremely dangerous and a huge red flag of drinking too much. If you drink to the point of a blackout, your body is telling you it cannot handle that amount of booze in that duration of time and it simply shuts all systems down to try and get the stuff out. Our bodies have an uncanny ability to take care of us, *if* we pay attention to the signals. Alcoholics, while actively drinking, also have an uncanny ability not to hear that voice inside telling us "when to say when." That popular phrase only works with you normal drinkers.

My first memorable blackout happened when I was 27. I woke up one morning and remembered I needed to fill my car with gasoline. It was close to empty when I had left the night before to go out. I get in my car and the gas tank is full! I must have stopped on my way home or maybe someone else took care of it for me, but it is still to this day, a total blackout. Just imagine what else could have happened? Another blackout occurred after an extremely hefty night of dozens of those jell-o shooters, you know the ones. They do taste great because it's jell-o with vodka (which has virtually no taste or smell), lots of vodka. The next morning I awake to find a cookie sheet on the stove with chocolate chip cookies stuck to the sheet and a pot of Uncle Ben's wild rice, not even touched but a spoon in it. Somehow I managed not to burn the apartment building down while trying to bake a midnight snack during my blackout. But the best part is that my clothes were drenched and in a pile on the den floor. How did they get wet? I had no idea. So I call my friend who I had been out with and he recounted the whole evening in a colorful depiction for me and seemed to have enjoyed watching me jump in the fountain in the middle of downtown! Now the last thing I remember from the previous evening was getting into a horse carriage. But I did drive myself home and attempted to cook and feed myself. At this point, one would think these incidents of serious, dangerous blackouts would cause me to stop or try to curb my drinking habits. But, no, I found they made for humorous (at the time) bar conversation.

The only relief from the symptoms of alcoholism is total abstinence. Just like the only sure way not to get pregnant, but easier said than done. Each year it became harder and harder to control the drinking because my mind and body were telling me I needed it more and more. Keep in mind, that while I was drinking, none of this occurred to me on a conscious level. All I knew was I wanted to drink, a lot. A good friend of mine summed it up in one word for me, *insidious*. I have to admit when I first heard this word I did not know the meaning of it. It sounded like one of those ugly words I probably would never use again, like frugal, but it caught my attention. So I looked up the definition in my dictionary: harmful yet beguiling. That's it, the meaning of *my* addiction to alcohol. I loved to drink, loved the people I drank with, the wonderful places it took me. All this was extremely attractive to me. Yet, when I drank, it took me to harmful, unhealthy places. I gave up all control of my life.

My decisions, my behavior, everything became under the influence and control of alcohol.

Sometime during the latter years of my drinking, it happened. Alcohol turned on me. My drinking had become insidious. My drinking episodes were no longer fun. It was more and more difficult to catch that "buzz." I seemed to just go straight to drunk without passing buzz. Alcohol lures us alcoholics in the beginning by making it all fun, then, once we are caught, the true nature of alcohol takes over. The game becomes insidious. I wanted control over alcohol. But I couldn't stop. What I did not realize at that point was my addiction was now in charge, forever.

Subconsciously, I knew all this. An alcoholic like me though will play ignorant as long as possible to this game called addiction. Most alcoholics will agree with me that you will do anything to try to stay in *control* of the drink, so as not to have to quit drinking altogether. Personally, I think this is the first sign of alcoholism. You try to "limit" the number of drinks at each outing, you plan to just drink "soft" liquor (whatever this is) like beer, stating, "no more shooters for me!" only to be buying rounds of shooters for everyone the following week. My personal favorite attempts at controlling my drinking were to wake up that next morning, after "who remembers" how many gin and tonics, with that kill-all hangover and swear (this is the good part), "I am NEVER drinking like that again!" I would even go so far as to throw all the liquor in the house down the drain. What a waste of money!! Because as soon as the pangs of hangover hell wore off, I was cussing myself as I drove to the liquor store, "why the hell did you throw all that good liquor away?" Insidious, isn't it?

Just as there are unique individuals in society, there are unique individual alcoholics. That critical turning point varies for each of us. Some experience it in their teens, some in their late-30's like me, some not until they are 50 or 60. Those are the ones I really despise, why couldn't I keep drinking until my 60's? Reminds me of those people who can eat everything in site and not gain an ounce. Just not fair is it? *When* this turning point hits us is not so important as the *recognition* of it. And this is where it gets hazy to explain because true, honest recognition only comes when we get sober. Until then, we would prefer to stay in that drunken subconscious domain where honesty and clarity are safely under cover and consequently won't make us feel like we need to stop drinking. Until sobriety, it is really all a mind game of control. The alcoholic monster in us wants to keep us drinking because its only goal is to destroy our bodies and lives. The alcoholic tries to control his drinking so that he does not have to quit drinking altogether. I fought it for more than 10 years before I decided I'd had enough of the fight. Before I realized I was the only one fighting. And that pain I had mentioned, my alcoholic companion also turned on it and left it all alone. My inner pain was all alone crying out in the darkness, allowing deceiving individuals to take advantage of its vulnerable heart, and exploring incredulously unsafe places in search of comfort and answers.

From that pain, the loneliness settled in. I could be in a room full of people and just feel all alone. Before, my bottle was the friend I could count on, but that friend was gone. That friend turned into a black cloud of distrust. Yet, I still yearned for the drink. I still tried over and over to get back with my trustworthy drinking companion. Then one day, I just gave up. I was tired. I was caught between a world of sanity that I once knew and this new world of total confusion and pain. I wanted out. I wanted my life back. The feeling of helplessness at that time was overwhelming. I did not know where to turn. I just knew I had to stop drinking. I wanted to stop drinking. So one morning I quit.

If I remember anything, it is *that* morning. On April 27, 1997, I was given a brand new birthday. It was a Sunday morning, my husband was gone and for the first time in my life I felt the pangs of loneliness. Not for my husband being gone, but for my soul, for my life. My whole body ached from bruises, emotional and physical. I remembered calling the police the night before, but by the time they arrived (two hours later), my husband had left on his own. I was a total wreck and had finally had enough of the battle with alcohol. It could win. But alcohol wouldn't have me. The first words out of my mouth were, "God, help me stop drinking." No words from me have ever or will ever carry more meaning, more raw sentiment. I was totally exhausted and totally helpless to stop drinking. That was my rock bottom. That is the place I hope and pray never to go back to. Because they say, if you do go back, you pick up exactly where you left off and it only gets worse from there. The only thing worse than that place for me would be hell.

Again, sobriety brings clarity. Once sober, you will *know* the time your alcohol took the fun away. You won't be able to mark the date on a calendar, but you'll recognize the time frame. You will also see how long you engaged in the battle. For me, it was about ten years. I didn't get sober until I was 37 years old. But the mind game didn't end just because I quit drinking. The alcoholic monster does not die, he just remains dormant, hoping for another opportunity to come back in full force. He plays with your mind. You think, "I've been sober a while now, I could just have one drink, that won't hurt." But it will hurt, you and so many others. So again, control is a huge factor. In sobriety, *we* must have the control.

For me, the act of getting sober meant taking the power of my addiction to control my drinking back. I constantly remind myself that relapse and eventual death is only one drink away. Being sober to me means the *only* thing I *need* to do each day is *choose* to not take a drink. How do I maintain my sobriety? That is plain and simple also. I pray. Every day.

At what point did the façade of my subconscious safety net break down and allow sanity to come in and slap me in the face? Why and at what breaking point, or that rock-bottom that most like to call it, did I decide to get sober? This point in my drinking life is just as important as the time when alcohol turned on me. It is even more difficult to explain because it involves the nature of spirituality. It is very difficult to describe or explain something intangible. How then, does one write about *feelings* that are indescribable? But that is my story. That is what happened to me when I got sober.

I had awoken many times before during my drinking years and said, "God, I will never drink like that again!" But the prayer on April 27th was different. I knew as I poured the remaining liquor in the house down the kitchen sink that I would not be making another trip to the liquor store. Don't ask me how I knew, something inside me just took over that morning and made me take care of no one but me. That something I now understand was the *Grace of God* awakening my soul. That is the *only* thing that could have made this alcoholic ask for help to stop drinking. My husband, friends, family all "suggested" I should quit, but that didn't matter to me. The only thing that mattered to me that morning was when I looked in the mirror and finally saw my true self. I finally accepted the face of alcoholism looking back at me. It was a face with a body that had no soul. And without a soul, my inner spirit had no place to breathe and live. I pray each day for the life of my soul.

I believe our spirits keep us alive from the inside out. It is where our passion for anything in life comes from. Our spirits have an incredible amount of healing power. That, I believe, is the main focus of our spirit, to heal our pain and to cleanse our mind, body, and soul from the ugliness in our world so that we never forget to feel the beauty, God's beauty. To never forget that God's beauty in life is life itself. Addictions are ugly. They strip away beauty in us and in our lives. My soul had been drowned in alcohol almost too long. But I now consider myself blessed to be an alcoholic, for had I not been an alcoholic and recovered, my journey would have been completely different. And this journey is filled with hope, love, song and dance. Yes, there is dancing again.

The spirit I found in myself thru my sobriety is the same spirit we all have as children, before we allow the demons to dance with us. Before we even know what demons are.

Most dictionaries define the word "addict" as someone who is devoted to a habitual or compulsive behavior. To use the word "devoted" presents a misconception. When I think of devoting myself to something, I think of consciously pursuing something out of a strong love and desire to acquire that something. What is missing in this concept of "devotion to a compulsive behavior" from an alcoholic's standpoint is an aspect of addiction that few understand.

That aspect is the deadly force of nature that drives an

alcoholic to continuously engage in self-destructive

behavior. Alcoholics are devoted to and love drinking. But,

this type of love and devotion is bred from a diabolical force.

And there is only one force greater than this deadly force of

nature and that is the force of God's grace.

If you are an alcoholic, you are the only one who can

give life back to your soul. Why do you think it is that you

often hate your drinking, hate what it does to you and your

loved ones? That feeling of hatred comes from your inner

spirit. Listen to it. For society is not responsible for saving

you, neither is your family. You alone are responsible, for

only you know when your spirit is calling. Choose to listen

and follow, for you may not be given another chance. There

is no greater freedom for an addict than the freedom felt at that moment of choosing to quit abusing. I know this because it happened to me.

My spiritual dance with life began once I got sober. This journey has made me aware of the simplest things in life, a new day without a hangover, sunshine, the mountains, rain, laughter, and especially, love. And love for myself. My most profound gratitude however, is for the awareness that God, my Higher Spirit, was always at my side through all those drinking years, keeping me safe.

One of the greatest gifts of my sobriety is having learned that turning to God for guidance is the only act of faith necessary to find my serenity. No matter what problems I may face, no matter what gifts are taken away, no matter how great the pain may feel, I know that I am never alone anymore in finding my way. That gift in and of itself is true peace to me and worth giving up the bottle for.

And now, the only deep-rooted pain I feel is for those

lonely addicts – some family, some friends, some unknown -

whose lives were lost before their peace was found on this

earth. Before they realized their dance was not over.

My Poems

I feel the loss of wasted
Yesterdays,
Swept away by the strength
Of a single desire

What of my today which an
Unsuspecting victim became?
Left alone to find strength in
Itself, by itself, for itself

Only a tomorrow can understand
The truth-
Accept the truth

Do not take away my sorrow
For in some strange way
My pain brings me peace

A peace that is completely
Mine – that is a part of
My soul that will not be shared

Without which the whole of
My being is not complete,
Not content nor secure

Utilize the energy that can be
Released from a deep-rooted pain for
Such heartaches should not be left to
Devour the soul

If I lived all alone in a house high
On a mountaintop
Would you come see me again?

If all my words were simple and
Sweet and nothing
Was said but what we really meant
Would you come see me again?

I have cried and I have bruised, now
Tired and weak
If I could only learn to stop living
In you – would you come see
Me again?

Cold – cold like the bitter wind
Seeping thru the pane,
Not seen yet keenly felt –
A shiver

There is no protection for a fear
Not understood
The dawn brings light and
Eases the darkness of
The night – or is it merely
Passage of time which
Calms the nerve?

Change is a constant

The one thing we can count
On in life, is change

Change in the seasons
Change in dress
Change in emotions once felt cause
Youthful desires and heartfelt
Dreams to diminish over time
Leaving only brick, stone and mortar
To remain against the
Forces of change

The bitter ice now melts
And the stifled
Greenery below blossoms

Smell the fresh, clean air filled
With sweet bubba,
Honeysuckle, and rose
Restrained almost too long

Such sweetness and warmth
Now to share again
Gone is the cold, for it was
Not too late

I feel my strength leaving
Very slowly diminishing
Into a realm where it
Shall never return

I am a dying soul, but no one
Can sense my pain
If only we could be like the
Greenery of this earth
That once a year is stilled by
The bitter cold of Winter –
Yet fearlessly, for such a death
Will only last until the
Nourishment of Spring returns

I felt the perfection in those
Wings outstretched
Prepared for flight

Such grace, freedom, serenity
And strength so finely
Enmeshed that distinction of one
Would scar the whole

Instinctively we strive for
Such completeness
Yet watch our lives drift away

Where would I go
Tomorrow if
My stars weren't in the
Sky tonight or the
Moon had lost its place?

I wake each morning
Knowing
All is going to remain
The same but
What if that bird
No longer sang?

What if all my plans
Were now
Memories and you
Became a part
Of my past?

In that moment of
Realization
That my norm will
Never again
Be what I know

Where will I go?

Just to see your smiling face
And smell the roses once more
Just to feel the sun warm your eyes
To share with those that pass you by

Our truth is long forgotten now,
Slowly as the seasons come and go
We felt it, held it for a time but
That was long ago

In a crowded room I am all alone,
Yet mingle with the senseless chatter
They smile, they drink, they laugh aloud
As my thoughts drift far away

Life is such a strange parade
I want to make my exit now,
But if I do, I will miss you most
Just to see your smiling face

Please smile for me once more

The wind blew and
The cardinals sang
All the while my
Heart cried out

Long days after longer
Nights of restless sleep
My thoughts scattered as
Each emotion beckoned

Beckoning a touch of
Warmth, an embrace
To behold the longing
Driven by the silent passion

Looking back is meaningless
Save to remind the
Heart of visions lost,
Memories not to be made

Suspended in time of
Hope and faith
For what passions are
Yet to be

For the flowers of spring
Have sprung again
Even though it is summer
And blown into
Tomorrow the storm clouds
We feared most

Our God is still there
Comforting our hearts
And souls like no other
Our prayers lifted up
By the angels of tender mercies

Where will our emotions
Take us now?
Now that the fear of
great loss escaped
Our hearts

All the desires of addiction
In my life
All the longing for love
Felt in my heart

Years of not knowing
Where, why
Sadness kept creeping
into my soul and
Leaving me empty
Then a voice reached
My heart
A voice of long ago
That would keep
Me safe when I believed

That voice was God
That voice was myself
That voice saved me
With it's perfection
Of timing and grace

For one more day
Would have taken
Me away forever into
A realm of constant
Sorrow and loss

One more day of
Tears would have
Drowned my spirit
And stained my
World with contempt
Instead of God's love
And simple happiness

In all the years of
Yearning for love
Thru all the days of
Wanting to know
The truth of love and
Faith and hope

Questioning each thought
Each feeling as true
When all the while
My heart ached
For the unknown passion
In life that keeps
Us endlessly searching

For God is truth and light
And glorious love
For God is faith and hope
That shines thru
Darkness without end

Yet that goodness is
Beyond our scope
Until the heart is lifted
By the spirit of
Grace and our soul no
Longer needs the search

Sinking into the
Hands of time
My memory fades as
Each sunrise approaches
To stretch my time
Further into tomorrow

A tomorrow not unlike
Many yesterdays
Yet for the unknown
That awaits
To create my future
Of sorrow and joy

For what is our life
But a memoir of
Repetitious thoughts and
Feelings and motions
Forging us into our
Realm of understanding,
Forgiving and accepting

My yesterday is a memory
Now and gone
Are the moments of passion
And desire of
Life and love

Only when I hear your
Voice does
Something stir inside
And remind me of
Yesterday's façade

I look in the mirror and
See a face I
No longer know and
The touch of
My skin is foreign and cold

Only tomorrow may wake
My senses and
Open the windows of life
And understanding

Only tomorrow may save
The pain and confusion
From my desperate mind and
set my longings free

Long ago I sat where the ocean
Meets the sand, closed
My eyes, listened

I heard seagulls flying over,
Calling me home
The depth of their cries
Louder and louder then
Softer as they called me home

Follow me, follow me to the
Place that is safe and
Warm – quiet yet full
Of laughter

I am finally going home, to
That place where the
Salt of the earth makes the
Earth – a never ending
Gentleness that comforts the soul
Where daytime is nighttime
And water is sand

Recognizable still is the face –
But no longer can it
Be shared, touched

A face weathered by one too
Many a bleak season
That washed away the soft
Compassion and gentle
Laughter that once flowed so
Freely form a heart too
Warm for it's own good

Left with the forced realization
That our strongest
Loves can bring forth our
Greatest pain

Your lovely spirit, beautiful
Carefree and untouchable
Felt only as a soft breeze
Against my cheek

And your quiet voice heard
Thru the rustle of
Autumn leaves turned red,
Gold, and orange by the
Sun's gentle rays

Gentle as your spirit that comforts
My soul when I feel all alone
Yet we are never alone, for our
Spirits are forever one

The sky is blue and the red bird
Sings – flying away
With your love

The sun is rising high and bright
Burning away
With your love

The road is long and narrow and
Steep – climbing away
With your love

The snow on the mountain still crisp
And white – melting away
With your love

Still they blossom and still they sing,
The water still clear and cold –
Why are my senses numb?

If I had known I could hold it
Not – would your love
Have gone

I went to the sea and thought
Of you today
And into the thick, salty air
All the lies were released
To be carried away – all of them
Forever

If only my pain could also be
Swept away
Or buried beneath the moistness of
The sand, far below until
No more is felt

Oh, how I loved you but told
You not, for then you would
Have left me sooner

And now as I stand alone
On this damp, windy morn, I
Say goodbye to you – and realize
I no longer have to live with
The lie that you were just my
Good friend

Where do the waters flow
Churning, rolling, foaming
Like the pounding of my breast
As I wait, yearning, fearing

A chilling breeze only
I can feel
Standing motionless, waiting
For yesterday to return

Words found written for
Me but now
Slowly paralyzing my soul
As my reality fades

Into a realm of darkness
Where my
Mind is torn by
Splintering lies

Thrashing the walls that
Bruise my skin
The whole of my life
Wanting to run,
To burn, to melt away
That truth

Then quiet and calm
As my senses
Realize we will never,
Can never
Go back

Now the beating of my
Heart forever stilled
When I followed my fears
And those simple
Words 'I Love You Too'
Appeared

Ice running thru
Veins felt as
His hand touched
Mine and the
Moment was silenced

Hands untouched by
Others as the fear
Of an unknown
Separated comfort to
The victims of pain

A pain unspoken
A pain born of and
Engulfed by the
Flame of indignation

Why is such a line
Drawn that shatters
The dignity of life,
Splintering love

Come into my heart
And remain there
For your love
Feeds my soul
To give
To all

Each day we awake with
Love, life and beauty
As possibilities to embrace
To share, to comprehend

I pray to my God above
For knowledge and insight
Not to ignore what are our
Spiritual gifts

For to not feel, to not breathe,
To not long for
A day of hope and laughter
Of sobriety and clarity
Is to not fully know Him

Believe in Your self
Where that Self comes from
Believe in that and that alone
Only your self and no one else

Stay in that place always
And you will be more than ok
You will rise above
You will fly with the phoenix
You will know your truth
And it will take you there

Always and forever

Believe

I don't want to wait
Until the sound of your voice
Is a memory or when
Your words spread no more
Joy and laughter

I don't want to wait until
Your breath is silenced
And your beautiful face
Has found its peace
With your Giver of spirit

I don't want to wait
Until you are gone to
Tell you what your life is to
Me every day of
My own fleeting existence

I need to tell you now
And often
Of the beauty you create
Just by being you

www.ingramcontent.com/pod-product-compliance
Lightning Source LLC
Chambersburg PA
CBHW032034090426
42741CB00006B/814